TURKISH CHILDREN'S BOOK

---

*Alice in Wonderland
(English and Turkish Edition)*

WAI CHEUNG

This page intentionally left blank.

ABOUT THE BOOK

Raise your children in a bilingual fashion with this bilingual coloring book that captures the magic and beauty of Alice in Wonderland's story along with a dual language storytelling that is perfect for parents who want to raise their children in a bilingual environment.

©Copyright, 2016, by Wai Cheung
All rights reserved.

CONTENTS

Plate 1. *Rabbit* 3

Plate 2. *Falling* 5

Plate 3. *The Caterpillar* 7

Plate 4. *Cheshire Cat* 9

Plate 5. *Tea Party* 11

Plate 6. *Painting Roses* 13

Plate 7. *The Queen* 15

Plate 8. *The Cards* 17

This page intentionally left blank.

Alice saw the White Rabbit pause for a moment to check the time on his pocket-watch.

Alice, Beyaz Tavşan'ın saate bakmak için cep saatine yönelerek bir süre durduğunu gördü.

Plate 1.
Rabbit

When the White Rabbit disappeared down a rabbit hole, Alice followed — and fell!

Beyaz Tavşan bir tavşan deliğinde kaybolduğunda, Alice de onu takip etti – ve düştü!

Plate 2.
Falling

Alice finally stopped falling, so she began to walk and encountered the Caterpillar.

Alice'in düşüşü sonunda durdu, ardından yürümeye başladı ve Tırtıl ile karşılaştı.

Plate 3.
The Caterpillar

She next met and looked up at the large grin of the Cheshire Cat.

Ardından Chesire Kedisiyle ve onun koca sırıtışıyla tanıştı.

Plate 4.
Cheshire Cat

Alice had tea with the very mad March Hare and Hatter, as well as the sleepy Dormouse.

Alice çılgın March Hare ve Hatter ile, ayrıca uykucu Dormouse ile birlikte çay içti.

Plate 5.
Tea Party

After the tiring tea party Alice saw three playing cards standing under a rose bush, ready to paint the white roses red.

Yorucu çay partisinden sonra Alice gül çalısının altında duran ve beyaz gülleri kırmızıya boyamaya hazır olan üç oyun kartı gördü.

Plate 6.
Painting Roses

Alice soon met the Queen of Hearts, who was quick to yell, "Off with her head!"

Alice kısa süre sonra ona "başını uçurun!" diye bağıran Kupa Kızı'nı gördü.

Plate 7.
The Queen

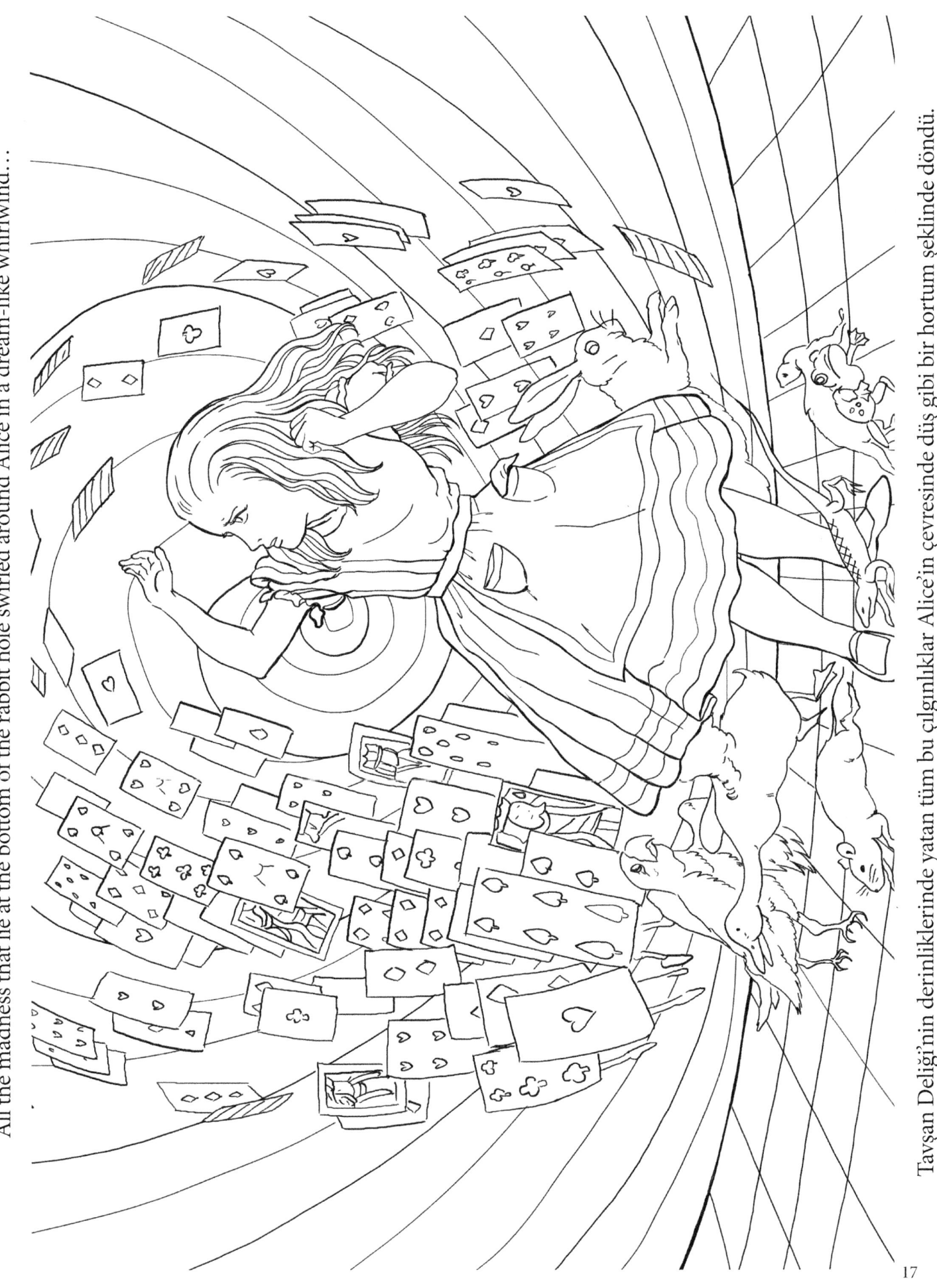

All the madness that lie at the bottom of the rabbit hole swirled around Alice in a dream-like whirlwind…

Tavşan Deliği'nin derinliklerinde yatan tüm bu çılgınlıklar Alice'in çevresinde düş gibi bir hortum şeklinde döndü.

Plate 8.
The Cards

ABOUT THE BOOK

Raise your children in a bilingual fashion with this bilingual coloring book that captures the magic and beauty of Alice in Wonderland's story along with a dual language storytelling that is perfect for parents who want to raise their children in a bilingual environment.

This page intentionally left blank.

Printed in Great Britain
by Amazon

Raise your children in a bilingual fashion with this bilingual coloring book that captures the magic and beauty of Alice in Wonderland's story along with a dual language storytelling that is perfect for parents who want to raise their children in a bilingual environment.

ISBN 9781533518613